BRIAN JOHNSTON

Esther – A Date with Destiny

Contents

I   Esther – A Date with Destiny

1   PREPARING TO MEET THE KING   3
2   BEAUTY IS MORE THAN SKIN-DEEP   10
3   ESTHER'S FINEST HOUR   16
4   ACCEPTED BY THE KING!   23
5   WHAT A DIFFERENCE A NIGHT MAKES!   29
6   A COMPLETE VICTORY   35

II   Joseph: Overcoming Life's Hurdles

7   OVERCOMING TENDENCY   43
8   OVERCOMING TEMPTATION   49
9   OVERCOMING DISAPPOINTMENT   54
10 OVERCOMING SUCCESS   60
11 OVERCOMING BITTERNESS   65

About the Publisher   71
About the Author   72
Also by Brian Johnston   73

I

Esther - A Date with Destiny

1

PREPARING TO MEET THE KING

The story of Esther is probably one of the most remarkable stories in the whole Bible. It has all the intrigue and as many twists as a modern thriller. Dark forces of evil, in opposition to the good, swirl around the lead character. She's a girl who is claimed by some Jewish sources to have been one of the four most beautiful women in the Bible. Others have classified the whole drama as a rags-to-riches (or even a peasant-to-princess) type of adventure. One thing's for sure, the Jewish girl Hadassah has more than a date with the king - it's a date with destiny. The stakes are high: the future of an entire nation hangs in the balance! A curious feature of the book, which is often commented upon, is that it lacks any direct mention of God. In the original Hebrew, the word for God can be found in acrostic form in the text; but in reality we hardly need to go to such lengths to find clear evidence of God's hand in the story that unfolds in this Bible book. We're left with every reason to believe that everything that happened was the design of divine Providence - or to put it another way, that God was behind everything that happened.

Although this book is a fascinating read for all ages, as well as being a favourite in Sunday Schools, I'd like to encourage us to read between the lines of the book of Esther. You certainly get the unmistakable impression that a sense of destiny is interwoven throughout all the varied circumstances by which Esther progresses. At first she's orphaned, then adopted, then she's selected for – and finally chosen by – the king of Persia to be his new queen. There may have been a thousand other contestants! Why was Esther chosen from an ethnic minority grouping across the vast Persian Empire? Was it simply mere chance? Was it simply because she was the most beautiful? Or was this her date with destiny? We're told that this last idea was her cousin's understanding of what was happening. It's my hope that as we explore this together, we'll be encouraged to reflect on how the hand of God is at work in the circumstances of our own lives. That's something even more thrilling than the book of Esther itself!

The story, as we'll see it unfold, is one in which Esther is enabled to find favour with the king (she pleases him) and then goes on to use that favour to achieve God's purpose for her people. Every believer on the Lord Jesus is in a position to recognize the grace (favour) God has already shown them and then, like the boy Jesus, to go on to *increase in favour with God* – the God who is the 'king eternal' (Luke 2:52; see 2 Peter 3:18; 1 Timothy 1:17). Was that promotion at work or that successful relocation purely down to our own efforts – or do we begin to sense the hand of God behind which there's a smiling Providence? If so, then the lesson of Esther is that we must prepare our hearts to discover the purpose towards which God is working in our lives. (None of this denies the fact that things may appear to go wrong in lives that please the Lord. Think of the extreme case of Job in the Bible. But that's beyond the scope of this book).

Without any further comment, let's launch ourselves into the story of Esther. We'll break in at chapter two – pausing only to say that chapter one has been a scene-setter explaining how the Persian king's queen, Vashti, had fallen into disfavour. The king has now had time to reflect...

"... when the anger of King Xerxes had subsided, he remembered Vashti and what she had done and what he had decreed about her. Then the king's personal attendants proposed "... Let the king appoint commissioners in every province of his realm to bring ... beautiful girls into the harem at the citadel of Susa. Let them be placed under the care of Hegai, the king's eunuch, who is in charge of the women; and let beauty treatments be given to them. Then let the girl who pleases the king be queen instead of Vashti." This advice appealed to the king, and he followed it. Now there was in the citadel of Susa a Jew of the tribe of Benjamin, named Mordecai ... who had been carried into exile from Jerusalem by Nebuchadnezzar king of Babylon ... Mordecai had a cousin name Hadassah, whom he had brought up because she had neither father nor mother.

This girl, who was also known as Esther, was lovely in form and features, and Mordecai had taken her as his own daughter when her father and mother died. When the king's order and edict had been proclaimed, many girls were brought to the citadel of Susa and put under the care of Hegai. Esther also was taken to the king's palace and entrusted to Hegai, who had charged of the harem. The girl pleased him and won his favour. Immediately he provided her with her beauty treatments and special food. He assigned to her seven maids selected from the king's palace and moved her and her maids into the best place in the harem ... Before a girl's turn came to go in to King Xerxes, she had to complete twelve months of beauty treatments prescribed for the women, six months with oil of myrrh and six with perfumes and cosmetics. And this is how she would go to the king: Anything she wanted was given to her to take with her from the harem to the king's palace" (Esther 2:1-13).

So far we've discovered that this Jewess, Esther (or Hadassah to call her by her Jewish name), had been orphaned and then adopted and now has been forcibly selected as a candidate in the contest to find the next queen of Persia. At first reading, that selection might seem to have a kind of fairy-tale glamour about it, but in reality it must have been very far from that. True, they probably received clothes, jewellery and perfumes to which they would otherwise never have had access – 'anything she wanted', the Bible says; but out of the possibly hundreds of girls only one would be chosen. The others might never see the king again, but they'd hardly be allowed to return to normal life. They would end up being retained in seclusion among the king's concubines. A Greek historian once described Xerxes as tall and handsome, but also as ruthless and jealous – one of the most formidable Persian Kings.

For one night with such a king – whom many of these girls had probably never seen before – each of them spent a full year in preparation. The twelve months of beauty treatments consisted of six months with oil of myrrh and six months with perfumes. In western culture perfume is splashed on in just a few moments. Obviously things were a bit different here! It appears that Persian women placed various scented oils on cosmetic coal-burners in order to perfume their skin and clothing. They would crouch over the burner with a robe draped over them like a tent. Even to this day wealthy Middle Eastern women will lay out their clothes over a latticework suspended over trays of fragrant incense burners. In this way the fragrance saturates their clothes.

Esther's first six months of preparation was with oil of myrrh. Although its smell is agreeable, the meaning of the word – as well as the taste of this substance – is bitter. In keeping with that, it has a definite Bible association with suffering (Mark 15:23) and death (John 19:39), being used as an anaesthetic and also for embalming the dead. These properties might suggest that there was an intended element of purification during those six months of being treated with myrrh. In fact, the word used for 'beautification' really means 'rubbing' - as in rubbing in the oils by way of purifying. Next came six more months of preparation – this time with the perfumes of sweet-smelling spices.

So overall it was a kind of bitter–sweet experience, and very extensive. In western culture at least, increasingly busy lives can often mean that people skimp on preparation. Lifestyle pressures make us look for instant results. This point in the story of Esther – where she prepares for twelve months for what in the first instance is only one night with the king – helps to challenge this. One thing led to another as God's purpose unfolded, and one day Esther would be able to look back on those twelve months as being time well spent.

Esther was caught up in God's amazing plan for her life. Her first meeting with the king was a critical part of that plan, and so the time laid down as required preparation wasn't wasted. Does it make us think about how little attention we give to important things – perhaps because of time that we have wasted on things that in the long run are not important – things outside of God's purpose for our lives? As Christians, our whole life is our preparation for the moment when we meet the King of kings, the Lord Jesus. Do we give enough attention to that? As we prepare for that, and as our lives please him, God will be working out his purpose in our lives at the same time. But how do we prepare ourselves? The Bible tells us to:

> *"lay aside the old self, which is being corrupted in accordance with the lusts of deceit …and put on the new self, which in the likeness of God has been created in righteousness and holiness of the truth"* (Ephesians 4:22–24 NASB).

Perhaps considering our body as dead to sin as we are taught to do in verses such as Colossians 3:5 and Romans 6:6,11 and mortifying its deeds (Romans 8:13) finds its parallel in the purifying with the bitter myrrh (with its association with death); and perhaps our displaying more and more the sweet aroma of the knowledge of Christ finds its parallel in Esther's preparation with sweet fragrances:

"Follow God's example, therefore, as dearly loved children and walk in the way of love, just as Christ loved us and gave himself up for us as a fragrant offering and sacrifice to God" (Ephesians 5:1-2).

"Now thanks be to God who always leads us in triumph in Christ, and through us diffuses the fragrance of His knowledge in every place. For we are to God the fragrance of Christ among those who are being saved and among those who are perishing" (2 Corinthians 2:14).

This is to be our lifelong preparation – as Christians – for our meeting with the King, if we're not to be ashamed before him at his coming (1 John 2:28). The hope of our meeting with the King of kings is to be a purifying hope (1 John 3:3). This is our destiny as believers: our own rags-to-riches story!

2

BEAUTY IS MORE THAN SKIN-DEEP

Let's pick up the story-line from where we left off in the previous chapter. We'll recap just a little, to the point where the king's agents are out searching for girls they considered to be suitable candidates to fill the vacant position of Queen of Persia:

> *"Mordecai had a cousin name Hadassah, whom he had brought up because she had neither father nor mother. The girl, who was also known as Esther, was lovely in form and features, and Mordecai had taken her as his own daughter when her father and mother died. When the king's order and edict had been proclaimed, many girls were brought to the citadel of Susa and put under the care of Hegai. Esther also was taken to the king's palace and entrusted to Hegai, who had charge of the harem. The girl pleased him and won his favour. Immediately he provided her with her beauty treatments and special food. He assigned to her seven maids selected from the king's palace and moved her and her maids into the best place in the harem. Esther had not revealed her nationality*

and family background, because Mordecai had forbidden her to do so. Every day he walked to and fro near the courtyard of the harem to find out how Esther was and what was happening to her." (Esther 2:7-20)

Here are the first indications of God's hand arranging things in Esther's favour. No sooner than she's introduced to Hegai, the man in charge of all the contestants, than she finds favour with him. As we'll see, that will prove a small, but helpful, step forwards in finding favour with the king as well. Because she pleases Hegai, he's prepared to accommodate her special dietary requirements. It's at this point that we might make a connection with the story of Daniel who, when he was brought as a captive to Babylon, also found favour, and was able to avoid food which he as a Jew would have objected to. Presumably, it's something similar here with the Jewess Hadassah when brought into the citadel of Susa. In a sense she was also a captive: she wasn't there of her own free will, but behind the will of the king's agents there was the sovereign will of Almighty God. We've just called her Hadassah, using her Jewish name, but she's best known to us by her Persian name, Esther, of course.

We're told that Esther was also given the best quarters, so that's another advantage. But even though things are going so well, now she's in grand surroundings with seven personal attendants, Esther doesn't suddenly acquire 'airs and graces.' We're told that she didn't reveal her nationality, because she still very much respected her cousin Mordecai's instructions. The words that describe Esther hint at a beauty within as well as describing her physical appearance. Her quiet, submissive spirit is very much part of the beauty God saw in her. The apostle Peter has something to say about this when in the third chapter of his first letter he writes:

> *"Wives, be submissive to your own husbands so that even if any of them are disobedient to the word, they may be won without a word by the behavior of their wives, as they observe your chaste and respectful behavior. Your adornment must not be merely external – braiding the hair, and wearing gold jewelry, or putting on dresses; but let it be the hidden person of the heart, with the imperishable quality of a gentle and quiet spirit, which is precious in the sight of God"* (1 Peter 3:1-4 NASB).

Esther showed just that kind of respectful behavior. She had her choice of gowns and jewellery, but her adornment was not limited to things that could be seen with the human eye. Esther's inner beauty of a gentle and quiet character already reflected the favour she'd found with God. Now we resume the contest to see who would find favour with the king of Persia:

> *"Before a girl's turn came to go in to King Xerxes, she had to complete twelve months of beauty treatments prescribed for the women, six months with oil of myrrh and six with perfumes and cosmetics. And this is how she would go to the king: Anything she wanted was given to her to take with her from the harem to the king's palace. In the evening she would go there and in the morning return to another part of the harem to the care of Shaashgaz, the king's eunuch who was in charge of the concubines. She would not return to the king unless he was pleased with her and summoned her by name.*

When the turn came for Esther (the girl Mordecai had adopted, the daughter of his uncle Abihail) to go to the king, she asked for nothing other than what Hegai, the king's eunuch who was in charge of the harem, suggested. And Esther won the favour of everyone who saw her." (Esther 2:12-15)

Did you notice how it was that Esther won the favour of all who saw her – including the king especially? It was because she was prepared to accept advice. I think the way it's put in the old Bible language hints that Esther had probably asked for the advice in the first place. That showed her wisdom, for she was from very humble circumstances compared to the rarefied atmosphere in which she was now moving. She would have been way out of her depth in all the protocol of the palace. But there was none of the arrogance of thinking that she knew best, which I'm sure would have characterized many of the other contestants when they suddenly had a blank cheque book with which to kit themselves out. Esther was wise to allow herself to be guided by this man. He would certainly know much more about the king's tastes and preferences than Esther did! The Bible book of Proverbs says: *"The wise listen and add to their learning ... the discerning get guidance ... But fools despise wisdom and discipline"* (Proverbs 1:5,7).

Esther – wise woman that she was – demonstrates here the characteristic that pleases God: that of being willing to accept advice, and to learn from others. There's nothing worse than a 'know-it-all' attitude in someone who simply can't be told. Once again, we're learning from Esther about the things that please God and open up the way for his purpose to be realized in our lives – just as it was in Esther's. For:

> *"She was taken to King Xerxes in the royal residence in the tenth month, the month of Tebeth, in the seventh year of his reign. Now the king was attracted to Esther more than to any of the other women, and she won his favour and approval more than any of the other virgins. So he set a royal crown on her head and made her queen instead of Vashti. And the king gave a great banquet, Esther's banquet, for all his nobles and officials. He proclaimed a holiday throughout the provinces and distributed gifts with royal liberality ... But Esther had kept secret her family background and nationality just as Mordecai had told her to do, for she continued to follow Mordecai's instructions as she had done when he was bringing her up."*

This is the most amazing example of the three we're looking at! The newly recognized Queen of Persia continued to follow Mordecai's instructions just as she'd done all the time he had been acting in the role of a father figure in her life. She was certainly fully obeying the spirit of the command: *"Honour your father and mother"!* (Exodus 20:12). She didn't stop just because she'd been made Queen. This reminds me of something even more amazing, something we read about in Luke's Gospel about Jesus as a boy. It's the time when he'd stayed behind at the temple without Mary and Joseph's knowledge:

> *"And he* [the boy Jesus] *said* [to Mary & Joseph], *"Why is it that you were looking for me? Did you not know that I had to be in My Father's house?" But they did not*

understand the statement which He had made to them. And He went down with them and came to Nazareth, and He continued in subjection to them; and His mother treasured all these things in her heart. And Jesus kept increasing in wisdom and stature, and in favour with God and men" (Luke 2:49-52).

Imagine the Son of God becoming subject to fallible human beings! But this is the way the Holy Spirit leads us to be pleasing to God (see Ephesians 5:21). For one of the ways in which it will be evident that we're 'filled with the Spirit' (Ephesians 5:18) will be when we're subject to one another in the fear of Christ. That's something that pleases God too, of course, and by increasing in favour with him – as Esther did with the king – we, too, may expect to find God honoring us, again as Esther was honoured. But let's learn from Esther that the benefits are not for us merely to indulge ourselves with, but for us to reinvest in reaching our appointed destiny.

3

ESTHER'S FINEST HOUR

The book of Esther traces how an orphaned Jewess gained access to the throne-room of a violent and pagan world-empire. We've seen how she found favour with king Xerxes of Persia, so much so that he chose her as his queen. Why Esther should be favoured in this way is an interesting question. She was evidently a very beautiful young woman and that at least ensured she qualified for the selection process when Xerxes was choosing his next queen. But as we read the Bible story more carefully, it comes across to us that Esther had an inner character which was beautiful in the sight of God. We've discovered she was patient and humble, with a teachable, submissive spirit; and God was very definitely at work in her life. God had designs on this young woman's life. I would suggest that Esther found favour with King Xerxes because she first had found favour with God. Our interest in this study is to observe how it was that Esther obtained that favour, so that we, too, can please the God who is himself the great King of the Ages.

In chapters 3 and 4 of the book of Esther the story takes a

dramatic turn. Destiny beckons for Esther. We are about to relive a life-and-death struggle at the heart of the Persian royal court, four centuries before Jesus Christ came to earth. We're about to discover why God has been pleased to oversee Esther's rise to royal position in the mighty Persian Empire. History would seemingly indicate that King Xerxes had personally led his troops into a disappointing invasion of Greece immediately after his marriage to Queen Esther. Some time went by before he returned to his palace at Susa. Perhaps the king's absence paved the way for one man to accumulate incredible power and influence. Chapter 3 tells us about him:

> *"After these events, King Xerxes honored Haman son of Hammedatha, the Agagite, elevating him and giving him a seat of honor higher than that of all the other nobles. All the royal officials at the king's gate knelt down and paid honor to Haman, for the king had commanded this concerning him. But Mordecai would not kneel down or pay him honor. Then the royal officials at the king's gate asked Mordecai, "Why do you disobey the king's command?" Day after day they spoke to him but he refused to comply. Therefore they told Haman about it to see whether Mordecai's behavior would be tolerated, for he had told them he was a Jew. When Haman saw that Mordecai would not kneel down or pay him honor, he was enraged. Yet having learned who Mordecai's people were he scorned the idea of killing only Mordecai.*

> *Instead Haman looked for a way to destroy all Mordecai's people, the Jews, throughout the whole kingdom of Xerxes ... Then Haman said to King Xerxes, "There is a certain*

people dispersed and scattered among the peoples in all the provinces of your kingdom whose customs are different from those of all other people and who do not obey the king's laws; it is not in the king's best interest to tolerate them. If it pleases the king, let a decree be issued to destroy them, and I will put ten thousand talents of silver into the royal treasury for the men who carry out this business." So the king took his signet ring from his finger and gave it to Haman son of Hammedatha, the Agagite, the enemy of the Jews. "Keep the money," the king said to Haman, "and do with the people as you please" (Esther 3:1-11).

Sadly there's nothing new about so-called ethnic cleansing. Haman had just succeeded in getting the king to authorize the extermination of the Jewish people. The only weapon in the arsenal of the Jewish people was the secret connection that they had to the king. For what Haman hadn't bargained for was that he'd just plotted against the king's bride. But Mordecai could take nothing for granted:

"When Mordecai learned of all that had been done, he tore his clothes, put on the sackcloth and ashes, and went out into the city, wailing loudly and bitterly. But he went only as far as the king's gate, because no-one clothed in sackcloth was allowed to enter it. In every province to which the edict and order of the king came, there was great mourning among the Jews, with fasting, weeping and wailing. Many lay in sackcloth and ashes ... Then Esther summoned [an attendant] ... to find out what was troubling Mordecai and why ... Mordecai told him

everything ... and he told him to urge her [Esther] *to go into the king's presence to beg for mercy and plead with him for her people"* (Esther 4:1-8).

Perhaps Mordecai at first thought Esther would be able to gain the king's ear more readily than others but Esther reminded him:

"All the king's officials and the people of the royal provinces know that for any man or woman who approaches the king in the inner court without being summoned the king has but one law: that he be put to death. The only exception to this is for the king to extend the gold scepter to him and spare his life. But thirty days have passed since I was called to go to the king" (Esther 4:11).

But Mordecai was insistent now. He'd not previously asked for Esther's intervention when the matter was personal between him and Haman, but now that the future of the whole nation hung in the balance, he lays it on the line:

"Do not think that because you are in the king's house you alone of all the Jews will escape. For if you remain silent at this time, relief and deliverance for the Jews will arise from another place, but you and your father's family will perish. And who knows but that you have come to royal position for such a time as this?" (Esther 4:13-14).

That was some speech, wasn't it? Winston Churchill, when addressing Britain to prepare it for a critical challenge during the

Second World War announced, "This is our finest hour!" Like the people of Britain, Esther rose magnificently to the occasion – inspired by the challenge that her finest hour had come. This was her date with destiny!

> *"Then Esther sent this reply to Mordecai: "Go gather together all the Jews who are in Susa, and fast for me. Do not eat or drink for three days, night or day. I and my maids will fast as you do. When this is done, I will go to the king, even though it is against the law. And if I perish, I perish"* (Esther 4:15-16).

Now it's the turn of Esther to demonstrate her faith in God. She called for a fast. When the Jews abstained from food like this, it was always associated with prayer. They fasted so as to make their voice to be heard on high (Isaiah 58:4). Whenever something was of such concern to them that they were prepared to go without food, they were proving their earnestness in the matter they were bringing before God. Esther knew the protocol of the king's court. In Persia, no-one could enter the inner court of the king unless they'd been invited – not even the queen. But Esther knew there was a higher court, the court of heaven. It was essential to access the court of heaven by prayer and fasting before attempting to enter the inner court of the king of Persia.

Having brought her petition first within heaven's court through prayer, she was then prepared to go against the law of Persia and enter the king's earthly court with her request to spare of the life of all her people. And she says, *"And if I perish, I perish."* By any standard these are remarkable words. She could still have entertained the notion that her royal position and secret identity would guarantee her personal safety despite Mordecai's warnings. But she chose to resign any possible rights of her own, and side with her people in order to intercede boldly for them.

This reminds me of something I've just been reading from Mark's Gospel chapter 8 about Jesus when he began to teach the disciples *"that the Son of Man must suffer many things and be rejected by the elders and the chief priests and the scribes, and be killed, and after three days rise again."* It was then that one of his disciples, Peter *"took Him aside and began to rebuke Him."* But Jesus *"rebuked Peter and said "Get behind Me, Satan; for you are not setting your mind on God's interests, but man's."* That was the occasion when he went on to speak about Christian discipleship in a very challenging way: *"If anyone wishes to come after me, he must deny himself, and take up his cross and follow me. For whoever wishes to save his life will lose it, but whoever loses his life for my sake and the gospel's will save it"* (Mark 8:31–35 NASB).

If Esther had not been prepared to put her life on the line, she would not have fulfilled the purpose for which God had been preparing her. In those tense scenes at the palace, Esther accepted she'd been favoured for a purpose. True, she'd pleased God, and he'd promoted her, but it was so that she might reinvest her earthly influence to do the will of heaven. And what about us? God has blessed us in every way spiritually. But to the extent he's also blessed us materially or advanced us to any position of influence, should we not consider his purpose in this?

If we're prepared to make it a matter of earnest prayer, and if we're ready to 'lose our life for His sake' – in other words, if we too, are prepared to put God's interests before our own interests, then who knows what will be the outcome of our life in the perspective of eternity? Mordecai pleaded with Esther not to 'remain silent.' If there's something we, too, are in a position to speak out about – in testimony for the Lord and about what's right – then let's be encouraged to do it even if it will mean loss of face or risking our reputation.

4

ACCEPTED BY THE KING!

Esther's people, the Jews, are doomed unless she can influence the king – but just getting safe access to him is far from guaranteed even to his queen! Historians say Xerxes became so angry when a storm once delayed the completion of a bridge during his Greek wars that he beheaded the men building it! If it's true that instability like that directed the vast power that was at his disposal, then Esther had every reason to fear for her own safety even though she was his queen! Esther had been queen for over a year by this time (Esther 3:7) and she'd now be familiar with the palace protocols. Remember she reminded Mordecai:

> *"All the king's officials and the people of the royal provinces know that for any man or woman who approaches the king in the inner court without being summoned the king has but one law: that he be put to death. The only exception to this is for the king to extend the gold scepter to him and spare his life. But thirty days have passed since I was called to go to the king"* (Esther

4:11).

It's likely that Esther could never be sure of her husband's state of mind. From sources outside the Bible we're told Xerxes was tall and handsome, but also violent and ruthless. Around the time Esther had been crowned queen, Xerxes had launched a major war against the Greeks (480 BC). Despite the king's personal leadership, the invasion had been disappointing. Memories of the Greek wars – and especially his humiliating defeat at the Bay of Salamis – could well having been preying on his mind. Apparently, the king had actually been sitting overlooking the bay, watching as his navy was surrounded and defeated before his eyes. Reversals like that would naturally have had a big influence on the king's mood.

Whatever the reason at this particular time, Esther hadn't been summoned into the king's presence for a whole month. To go in now – uninvited – was courting danger. Maybe thoughts of her predecessor, Queen Vashti, passed through her mind. Vashti had offended the king by refusing to come to him when invited; now Esther was considering going to the king uninvited – that, too, could prove to be a fatal mistake. Despite her misgivings, Mordecai, whose advice she followed, had replied:

> *"Do not think that because you are in the king's house you alone of all the Jews will escape. For if you remain silent at this time, relief and deliverance for the Jews will arise from another place, but you and your father's family will perish. And who knows but that you have come to royal position for such a time as this?"* (Esther 4:13,14).

Hers was a dangerous destiny. The Persian royal palace at Susa, in modern south-west Iran, was not a safe place for anyone. Even kings were paranoid of would-be assassins. We can be pretty sure that's why uninvited access to the king was so strictly controlled - at peril of death. So there seemed to be danger on all sides for Esther: Haman was the highly placed enemy of her people, but also no place was more dangerous than being on the wrong side of the king. But Esther made up her mind: she would go to the king. First, she prepared herself by entering the court of heaven's King through fasting and (we can safely assume) through prayer. Then she took her first steps towards entering uninvited into the king's inner court. There's a palpable sense of tension as we turn to chapter five of the book of Esther:

> *"On the third day Esther put on her royal robes and stood in the inner court of the palace, in front of the king's hall. The king was sitting on his royal throne in the hall, facing the entrance. When he saw Queen Esther standing in the court, he was pleased with her and held out to her the gold scepter that was in his hand. So Esther approached and touched the tip of the scepter. Then the king asked, "What is it, Queen Esther? What is your request? Even up to half the kingdom, it will be given you"* (Esther 5:1-3).

The only way in which the death sentence could be over-ruled was if the king held out the golden scepter. What a tremendous relief it must have been for Esther – to see that scepter being extended towards her. It was the sign that she'd been accepted! She'd survived her life-and-death encounter with the king! In a way I'm reminded of God's instructions to the Israelites long before in the days of Moses. To Moses he'd said, *"No man can see Me and live"* (Exodus 33:20); and to Aaron, Moses' brother, and the high priest, God said that once a year:

> *"He shall take a fire pan full of coals of fire from upon the altar before the LORD and two handfuls of finely ground sweet incense, and bring it inside the veil. He shall put the incense on the fire before the LORD that the cloud of incense may cover the mercy seat that is on the ark of the testimony, otherwise he will die"* (Leviticus 16:12-13).

The danger involved in Esther's journey into the king's inner sanctum was down to fickleness of human character; but the danger for Israel's high priest in that carefully regulated and limited access into the inner sanctum of God's earthly house was as a result of the holiness of God. What a contrast all this is with the great news God has for us in the New Testament! It's not that God's changed; that's impossible. The difference is down to the work which God's Son, Jesus Christ, has done for us. He came and died as a sacrifice upon the cross so that you and I might be justified – a simple way of understanding that important Bible word is to read it as "just-as-if-I'd never sinned." In Romans chapter 5, the apostle Paul says: *"Therefore, having been justified by faith, we have peace with God through our Lord Jesus Christ, through whom also we have access by faith into this grace in which we stand"* (vv. 1-2 NKJV).

Notice, will you, the word 'access': the access to God which believers enjoy. Again, in writing to the church of God at Ephesus, Paul addressed Gentiles whom he described as being 'afar off' from God, as well as addressing Jews whom he described as near, and he spoke of how Jesus Christ: *"... came and preached peace to you who were afar off, and to those who were near. For through him we both* [Gentiles and Jews now] *have access by one Spirit to the Father"* (Ephesians 2:17-18 NKJV). That's the same word 'access' again. Then, in the next chapter he says *"... Christ Jesus our Lord, in whom we have boldness and access with confidence through faith in Him"* (Ephesians 3:11-12 NKJV).

I'm sure you've previously noticed the repetition of the word 'access' in all these verses – but these are the only places in the New Testament where we find this word 'access': it's a word meaning 'approach' or 'introduction' – perhaps best summed up by the French word 'entrée.' Originally, the Bible word 'access' referred to the act of a person who secured an interview with a king on behalf of someone else. In the first place the person who secured the interview would himself need to be close to the king. Now as the apostle Paul uses it these three times in the Bible, the person who acts for us to allow us access to God the Father is of course the Lord Jesus.

Since he occupies the closest place in the Father's affections as God's own well-beloved Son, he's ideally fitted for this task on our behalf. There was also a second idea in this Bible word 'access'. The person for whom the access or entrée to the king has been gained must himself – or herself – be acceptable to the king. That, of course, is what the Lord Jesus did for us through the blood of his cross where he put away our sin by the sacrifice of himself. He took our sin and he gave us his righteousness! That's the wonderful exchange which is at the very heart of God's Good News for each one of us.

That exchange of our sin for his righteousness becomes effective only when we put our trust in God's Son, Jesus Christ. When we believe on the Lord Jesus Christ, at that very moment we receive his righteousness – his perfect standing before the throne. Clothed in his righteousness we become 'accepted in the Beloved' (Ephesians 1:6 NKJV). I was recently thinking how it's even more wonderful than that. Not only do we have Christ's own righteousness given to us to make us acceptable to God (acceptable in that we become as righteous as Christ is himself!), but we also have his preciousness given to us as well! The apostle Peter tells us this in First Peter 2 verse 7: "*To you therefore that believe is the preciousness.*" So we're as precious to God as Jesus is! The preciousness of Jesus in the eyes of his Father has been given (or imputed) to us just as his righteous standing before God has been given to us. This is the glory of the Gospel of God's grace!

Think once more of Esther bringing Mordecai's appeal before the king. Unlike Mordecai and Esther we no longer have any fear of entering God's presence at any time with our prayer requests; nor need we feel anything other than boldness to come before heaven's eternal King as part of a worshipping people. But let's be reminded that that's an amazing privilege, secured for us through our Lord Jesus. Did he not say to disciples who remain in him: "*So that whatever you ask of the Father in My name He may give to you*" (John 15:16). Praise God we have a permanent entrance which by faith, and the name and person of Jesus is our golden scepter which grants the acceptance of our requests!

5

WHAT A DIFFERENCE A NIGHT MAKES!

Esther's identity is still secret, but her people, the Jews, are doomed unless she can influence the king. So far so good: Esther has survived a daring breach of royal protocol by arriving uninvited in the king's presence. As soon as she knew the king had favoured her – by granting her an audience – we might think Esther would get straight to the point. After all, the stakes were so high: the lives of all her people are hanging in the balance. But Esther didn't immediately blurt out the problem that troubled her so much. No, when the king asked:

> *"What is it, Queen Esther? What is your request? Even up to half the kingdom, it will be given you." "If it pleases the king," replied Esther, "let the king, together with Haman, come today to a banquet I have prepared for him." "Bring Haman at once," the king said, "so that we may do what Esther asks." So the king and Haman went to the banquet Esther had prepared"* (Esther 5:3-5).

Half the kingdom of Persia was a generous offer! When Alexander the Great finally conquered Persia and entered Susa perhaps a hundred years later, he was dazzled by all the wealth he found. It was reported at twelve hundred tons of gold and silver bullion along with two hundred and seventy tons of minted gold coins accumulated by the Persian kings! But Esther wasn't a gold-digger. From what we've learnt of her and her purpose, we're probably prepared for Esther to reject the offer of half the kingdom, but all she requests instead is the king's company! She requested the king's company, along with Haman, his prime minister, at a special meal that she was going to prepare. We might have expected her straightaway to beg for the deliverance of her people who were ensnared in the prime minister's evil plot against them. But no, she didn't. What amazing restraint she showed by not immediately presenting her problem!

When we enter into God's presence in prayer, do we perhaps struggle with the tendency to immediately pour out our requests, detailing all our problems, and maybe those injustices done against us? Of course, there's nowhere better to bring our difficulties, than before God's throne. But which is more important: the instant relief of unburdening ourselves, or first showing respect for God by appreciating his greatness and the glory of our relationship to him? Isn't this how the Lord Jesus himself has taught us to pray:

> *"Our Father who is in heaven, Hallowed be Your name. Your kingdom come. Your will be done, on earth as it is in heaven. Give us this day our daily bread. And forgive us our debts, as we also have forgiven our debtors. And do not lead us into temptation, but deliver us from evil. For*

*Yours is the kingdom and the power and the glory forever.
Amen"* (Matthew 6:9–13 NASB).

Notice the attention that is paid first to God's name and kingdom
and will, before any mention of our needs – which, of course,
God already knows about well before we come to him. So maybe
we can take Esther's action as a reminder to us that we should
make sensing God's presence and adoring his greatness our very
first focus in prayer. Whenever we seek his face we want first of
all to just enjoy his company. So back to Esther again, as she now
entertains the king and Haman who have come as she requested:

> *"As they were drinking wine, the king again asked Esther,
> "Now what is your petition? It will be given you. And
> what is your request? Even up to half the kingdom, it will
> be granted." Esther replied, "My petition and my request
> is this: If the king regards me with favour and if it pleases
> the king to grant my petition and fulfill my request, let
> the king and Haman come tomorrow to the banquet I will
> prepare for them. Then I will answer the king's question"*
> (Esther 5:6–8).

Once again Esther invites the king for a meal. She wants to
spend yet more time in his company before she makes her appeal.
I wonder if we can take that as another reminder of how our
King wants us to invite his company, and longs for us to have
unhurried fellowship with him – instead of our rushing in and
out of his presence with a kind of shopping list our requests.
It's in Revelation 3 and verse 20 that he says: *"Behold, I stand at
the door and knock; if anyone hears my voice and opens the door,
I will come in to him and will dine with him, and he with me."*

In the story of Esther, she was alone with the king – well, not quite alone! Haman, the prime minister was there too! I don't suppose Haman ever considered what he was supposed to be doing there in those intimate banquets. He was just too full of himself …

> *"Haman went out that day happy and in high spirits. But when he saw Mordecai at the king's gate and observed that he neither rose nor showed fear in his presence, he was filled with rage against Mordecai … His wife Zeresh and all his friends said to him, "Have a gallows built, seventy-five feet high, and ask the king in the morning to have Mordecai hanged on it. Then go with the king to the dinner and be happy." This suggestion delighted Haman, and he had the gallows built"* (Esther 5:9,14).

But in a glorious irony of divine providence, the very same evening Haman was plotting his revenge against Mordecai; King Xerxes was that very same night pacing the palace floor with royal insomnia, for chapter six opens with the words:

> *That night* [that night of all nights!] *the king could not sleep; so he ordered the book of the chronicles, the record of his reign, to be brought in and read to him. It was found recorded there that Mordecai had exposed Bigthana and Teresh, two of the kings's officers who guarded the doorway, who had conspired to assassinate King Xerxes. "What honor and recognition has Mordecai received from this?" the king asked. "Nothing has been done for him," his attendants answered"* (Esther 6:1-3).

What a difference a single night can make! This was no coincidence! No one but God knows why Mordecai's good deed wasn't rewarded immediately, but historians tell us that King Xerxes was busy warring against the Greeks around the time Esther was crowned queen, so that could have been ground enough for distraction. But in any case we can see the hand of God in all this.

Right now, I just want to pause to remind us all as Christians that we serve a God who never slumbers – a God who records all our service before him, and in his time he will reward us. Almost the last words of the Bible are: *"Behold, I am coming quickly, and My reward is with Me, to render to every man according to what he has done"* (Revelation 22:12). But let's return to where we interrupted the story of Esther. A new day is dawning in the royal palace at Susa:

> *"The king said, "Who is in the court?" Now Haman had just entered the outer court of the palace to speak to the king about hanging Mordecai on the gallows he had erected for him. His attendants answered, "Haman is standing in the court." "Bring him in," the king ordered. When Haman entered, the king asked him, "What should be done for the man the king delights to honor?" Now Haman thought to himself, "Who is there that the king would rather honor than me?" So he answered the king, "For the man the king delights to honor, have them bring a royal robe the king has worn and a horse the king has ridden, one with a royal crest placed on its head.*
>
> *Then let the robe and horse be entrusted to one of the*

king's most noble princes. Let them robe the man the king delights to honor, and lead him on the horse through the city streets, proclaiming before him, 'This is what is done for the man the king delights to honor!" "Go at once," the king commanded Haman. "Get the robe and the horse and do just as you have suggested for Mordecai the Jew, who sits at the king's gate. Do not neglect anything you have recommended." So Haman got the robe and the horse. He robed Mordecai, and led him on horseback through the city streets, proclaiming before him, "This is what is done for the man the king delights to honor!" Afterwards Mordecai returned to the king's gate.

But Haman rushed home, with his head covered, in grief, and told Zeresh his wife and all his friends everything that had happened to him. His advisers and his wife Zeresh said to him, "Since Mordecai, before whom your downfall has started, is of Jewish origin, you cannot stand against him – you will surely come to ruin!" While they were still talking with him, the king's eunuchs arrived and hurried Haman away to the banquet Esther had prepared" (Esther 6:4-14).

So we are set up for the great reversal that takes place in the story of Esther: the reversal of Haman's fortunes – the downfall has begun of this great enemy of God's people. From the list of honors which Haman at first thought he was putting forward for himself, it could almost seem as though he had ambitions to be king. It might even make us think of Lucifer who wanted to set his throne above God's. In fact that parallel can be extended a bit further as we hope to show in the next chapter.

6

A COMPLETE VICTORY

The book of Esther is more than a story of palace intrigue, abduction, murder, assassination plots, genocide and impossible romance on the edge of life and death. One writer has noted that the Nazis banned anyone from reading it in the concentration camps. It's an unforgettable book that demonstrates Jewish resistance to annihilation. We've now reached the point in the unfolding drama where Queen Esther reveals her Jewish identity and exposes Haman's plan to exterminate the Jews as being a personal attack on her and her people. Esther has waited to choose her moment at the second of two private banquets with the king and Haman, the prime minister:

> *"... the king and Haman went to dine with Queen Esther, and as they were drinking wine on that second day, the king again asked, "Queen Esther, what is your petition? It will be given you. What is your request? Even up to half the kingdom, it will be granted." Then Queen Esther answered, "If I have found favour with you, O king, and if it pleases your majesty, grant me my life – this is*

my petition. And spare my people – this is my request"
(Esther 7:1-3).

Esther's request was very much to the point; "Grant me my life – this is my petition." My petition is my life, she says! We too, have a great Adversary, the Devil or Satan. And he's out to spoil our lives. He wants to render them useless as far as our serving God is concerned. Thinking about that makes us realize that the most important prayer request we, too, can make to God is that he'll save our life from our great enemy – this is the very prayer that Jesus said he had made on behalf of his disciple, Peter (Matthew 6:13). We long that God will preserve our lives for his service. But before we go any further into that let's first hear King Xerxes reaction to Esther's startling request:

"King Xerxes asked Queen Esther, "Who is he? Where is the man who dared to do such a thing?" Esther said, "The adversary and enemy is this vile Haman." Then Haman was terrified before the king and queen. The king got up in a rage, left his wine and went out into the palace garden. But Haman realizing that the king had already decided his fate, stayed behind to beg Queen Esther for his life. Just as the king returned from the palace garden to the banquet hall, Haman was falling on the couch where Esther was reclining. The king exclaimed, "Will he even molest the queen while she is with me in the house?" As soon as the word left the king's mouth, they covered Haman's face. Then Harbona, one of the eunuchs attending the king, said, "A gallows seventy-five feet high stands by Haman's house. He had it made for Mordecai, who spoke up to help the king." The king said, "Hang him on it!"

*So they hanged Haman on the gallows he had prepared
for Mordecai. Then the king's fury subsided"* (Esther
7:5-10).

Haman had fatally over–reached himself. He'd tried to engineer the death of Mordecai on these gallows, but instead he'd sealed his own fate. There's a very wonderful parallel here. The enemy of God, Satan, put it into Judas' heart to betray Jesus to the authorities so that he might suffer death on a cross. But the Bible tells us that the God whose hand we see at work in the book of Esther was also at work in the great drama of the cross. The Bible tells us that Jesus was *"... delivered over by the predetermined plan and foreknowledge of God,* [and the apostle Peter says to the Jews at that time] *you nailed [Him] to a cross by the hands of godless men and put Him to death. But God raised Him up again, putting an end to the agony of death, since it was impossible for Him to be held in its power."* (Acts 2:23,24) According to later in the Bible, this predetermined plan of God was *"... that through death He [Jesus] might render powerless him who had the power of death, that is, the devil, and might free those who through fear of death were subject to slavery all their lives"* (Hebrews 2:14-15).

Just as they hanged Haman on the gallows he had prepared for Mordecai – turning his own weapon against him – so Satan, by having Jesus betrayed and so put to death, actually sealed his own fate, because by that death on the cross two thousand years ago Jesus rendered powerless the Devil and the very power of death itself for all who believe on him. Satan's own weapon of death was turned against him to defeat him! However, back in the story of Esther, Haman has been put to death on his own gallows, but his plan still lives on because it had had the king's unchangeable seal of approval at the time. There's still work for Esther to do as we see as we read on:

> *"That same day King Xerxes gave Queen Esther the estate of Haman, the enemy of the Jews. And Mordecai came into the presence of the king, for Esther had told how he was related to her. The king took off his signet ring, which he had reclaimed from Haman, and presented it to Mordecai. And Esther appointed him over Haman's estate. Esther again pleaded with the king, falling at his feet and weeping. She begged him to put an end to the evil plan of Haman the Agagite, which he had devised against the Jews"* (Esther 8:1-3).

It's interesting that Haman is described as an Agagite. It raises the possibility that this man was a descendant from the Amalekite king of that name, king Agag, whose life Saul had at first spared when he'd really been commanded to destroy all the Amalekites (1 Samuel 15:3). It could be that Queen Esther is finishing off the job that king Saul had signally failed to do – and which, as a result of Saul not doing it, had brought the future of the Jewish people into real jeopardy at this time. Of one thing we can be sure: it's the things we leave undone, that often become our own undoing. Let's take that lesson to heart! As we've said Haman's plan lived on. A command in the king's name had been issued to destroy all the Jews, and according to Persian custom any command in the king's name could not be changed once it had been issued. What could be done? Esther proposes a solution by asking the king to issue a second edict or command:

"If it pleases the king," she said, "and if he regards me with favour and thinks it the right thing to do, and if he is pleased with me, let an order be written overruling the dispatches that Haman son of Hammedatha, the Agagite, devised and wrote to destroy the Jews in all the king's provinces..." King Xerxes replied, "... write another decree in the king's name on behalf of the Jews as seems best to you, and seal it with the king's signet ring – for no document written in the king's name and sealed with his ring can be revoked..." The king's edict granted the Jews in every city the right to assemble and protect themselves; to destroy, kill and annihilate any armed force of any nationality or province that might attack them and their women and children; and to plunder the property of their enemies..." (Esther 8:5-11).

So Haman's command which had also been in the king's name couldn't be withdrawn or suspended, but a second command could be given also in the king's name which gave the Jews the right to self-defense – and with the encouragement of the king's command behind them now, they certainly did that, as we read ...

"On the thirteenth day of the twelfth month, the month of Adar, the edict commanded by the king was to be carried out. On this day the enemies of the Jews had hoped to overpower them, but now the tables were turned and the Jews got the upper hand over those who hated them. The Jews assembled in their cities in all the provinces of Xerxes to attack those seeking their destruction. No-one could stand against them ..." (Esther 9:1,2).

At this point the Jews were safe; they had gained the victory over their enemies. In the citadel of Susa alone, the Jews had killed and destroyed five hundred men and ten sons of Haman. Surely Esther and Mordecai are satisfied. But no, Esther has a further request to ask of the king:

> *"If it pleases the king," Esther answered, "give the Jews in Susa permission to carry out this day's edict tomorrow also, and let Haman's ten sons be hanged on gallows." So the king commanded that this be done. An edict was issued in Susa, and they hanged the ten sons of Haman. The Jews in Susa came together on the fourteenth day of the month of Adar, and they put to death in Susa three hundred men, but they did not lay their hands on the plunder"* (Esther 9:13-15).

Esther was ensuring a complete victory! We've been applying lessons about seeking God's help to preserve our lives in his service – we can never fall away from our salvation; but it's possible for us to fall away from serving God according to his will and in the way that gives him pleasure. We've also been thinking about how, as Christians, we shouldn't leave undone things which will later become our undoing – as King Saul did. Rather, we should put to death what God has asked us to put to death: we should mortify the deeds of our sinful nature (Colossians 3:5), and with God's help seek a total victory over the lusts which war against our souls (1 Peter 2:11). Not that we'll ever reach sinless perfection this side of heaven, but it's God's purpose for our lives that we live in the fullness of the victory the Lord Jesus gained for us through his death on the cross.

II

Joseph: Overcoming Life's Hurdles

7

OVERCOMING TENDENCY

Have you ever been let down by someone? When it's someone you've every reason to expect to be reliable, it's all the harder to take; especially if it's a relative or close family friend who betrays your trust. The Bible story of Joseph, recorded in the Bible's first book of Genesis, serves as an extreme example of this. Let's refresh our memories on the story line:

> *"Joseph, when seventeen years of age, was pasturing the flock with his brothers while he was still a youth, along with the sons of Bilhah and the sons of Zilpah, his father's wives. And Joseph brought back a bad report about them to their father. Now he* [Jacob] *loved Joseph more than all his sons, because he was the son of his old age; and he made him a varicolored tunic. And his brothers saw that their father loved him more than all his brothers; and so they hated him and could not speak to him on friendly terms. Then Joseph had a dream, and when he told it to his brothers, they hated him even more. And he said to them, "Please listen to this dream which I have had;*

for behold, we were binding sheaves in the field, and lo, my sheaf rose up and also stood erect; and behold, your sheaves gathered around and bowed down to my sheaf." Then his brothers said to him, 'Are you actually going to reign over us? Or are you really going to rule over us?" So they hated him even more for his dreams and for his words ...

And his brothers were jealous of him, but his father kept the saying in mind. Then his brothers went to pasture their father's flock in Shechem. And he [Jacob] said to Joseph, "Are not your brothers pasturing the flock in Shechem? Come, and I will send you to them. "And he said to him, "I will go." Then he said to him, "Go now and see about the welfare of your brothers and the welfare of the flock; and bring word back to me." ... When they saw him from a distance and before he came close to them, they plotted against him to put him to death. And they said to one another, "Here comes this dreamer!" Now then, come and let us kill him and throw him into one of the pits; and we will say, A wild beast devoured him.' Then let us see what will become of his dreams!"...

So it came about, when Joseph reached his brothers, that they stripped Joseph of his tunic, the varicolored tunic that was on him; and they took him and threw him into the pit. Now the pit was empty, without any water in it. Then they sat down to eat a meal ... Then some Midianite traders passed by, so they pulled him up and lifted Joseph out of the pit, and sold him to the Ishmaelites for twenty shekels of silver. Thus they brought Joseph into Egypt...they took

Joseph's tunic, and slaughtered a male goat, and dipped the tunic in the blood; and they sent the varicolored tunic and brought it to their father and said, "We found this; please examine it to see whether it is your son s tunic or not." Then he examined it and said, "It is my son's tunic. A wild beast has devoured him; Joseph has surely been torn to pieces!" So Jacob tore his clothes, and put sackcloth on his loins, and mourned for his son many days. Then all his sons and all his daughters arose to comfort him, but he refused to be comforted" (Genesis 37:2–35).

Jacob's actions within the family circle had certainly created an inflammable atmosphere. He had taken multiple wives, and then singled one out as his favourite. He'd then further singled out one of her children as being the special object of his affections. What's more, he'd done this in a very public way (giving Joseph that special coat) which was a totally inappropriate signal to the other siblings. It seems Jacob couldn't have stoked up the fires of jealousy any better if he'd tried! There's also a hint that Jacob might even have used Joseph as something of a spy to report back to him on his brothers' misdemeanours. If all that created the inflammable atmosphere, then Joseph himself generated the sparks.

In addition to what could be construed as tale-telling about his brothers, it would seem Joseph showed gross insensitivity in broadcasting the interpretation of his dreams. He seemed oblivious as to how explosive the whole situation was becoming. None of this, of course, justifies or even excuses what his brothers did to him. To sell your own brother (or half-brother) into a life of slavery and cover it up by faking his death was a horrible act of treachery. But the real lesson for us is how Joseph overcame this treachery. It was a tough hurdle for a 17-year-old to clear, but he did it and developed character in all the adversity he went through.

Abraham Lincoln, the sixteenth president of the United States, said that it's not so much adversity that's a test of man's character as what he does when he's in a position of power. I think there's a lot of truth in that. Joseph develops character here in adversity, then goes on to display it later when he's finally in a position of power - as God promised he would be one day through the dreams Joseph experienced. It says in Psalm 105, that the Word of God tested Joseph. God had revealed his Word to Joseph early in life through his dreams which promised he'd hold high office, but so much was about to go wrong for Joseph that he'd have every opportunity to doubt the reality of these promises. Yet there's no indication that he did.

As we come to the end of the chapter, it's only Joseph who seems to remain unruffled and serene. Jacob is in mourning and great distress, and his brothers were surely, even at this stage, beginning to be tortured by their guilt (see Genesis 42:22). Of course, Joseph had begged for mercy and pleaded with his brothers at the time, but there's never even the slightest hint of him afterwards becoming bitter in his attitude towards them. Doesn't this illustrate the kind of response to adversity that the apostle Peter encouraged in the first century Christians he was writing to, when he said: *"... now for a little while, if necessary, you have been distressed by various trials, that the proof of your faith, being more precious than gold which is perishable, even though tested by fire, maybe found to result in praise and glory and honor at the revelation of Jesus Christ"* (1 Peter 1:6-7).

Peter has already spoken of the promised inheritance that awaits Christian believers in heaven, but he goes on to recognize that adversity must often be faced first in this life. At times it may be the adversity of treachery. Joseph passed the test. There's no indication that he ever doubted his dreams or disbelieved the Word of God to him despite his adverse circumstances. The Christian who's mistreated by others can allow that to be like God's fire which refines their character as they keep unwavering faith in future blessing promised by God. Such mistreatment that we may be called upon to endure can surely never be God's will for the perpetrators; but it may be God's will for us. By passing through it we should develop a more complete, more rounded Christian character. Paul says in Romans 15 that tribulation brings about perseverance and perseverance proves character (vv.3-4).

The Lord Jesus himself faced the trial of treacherous betrayal by one of his own disciples. The Bible even goes so far as to describe Judas as Jesus' 'own familiar friend.' Isn't the very epitome of treachery the kiss with which Judas betrayed his master in the garden of Gethsemane? But then the Lord went onwards to the cross so that we who believe in him can share his triumph. We can experience something of what the hymn writer described poetically as the cross sweetening 'every bitter cup.'

As with Joseph, even treachery can make us better instead of bitter! Rejoicing in God's forgiveness for ourselves through the cross, we can learn to forgive others too. Is there a former friend or perhaps a family member who's misused you – someone you need to reach out to again? Like King David in desire to do good to the family of Saul which had done such evil to him, you, too, have an opportunity to demonstrate the amazing 'kindness of God.'

8

OVERCOMING TEMPTATION

Success doesn't come on its own. It brings temptations with it. Some newspapers appear to be full of scandals involving people in the public eye who in their private lives have allegedly succumbed to temptation. When it concerns sports personalities and media celebrities, a contributory factor is usually the fact that these people are having to handle all the attention that fame and great wealth brings at a relatively young age. For many, apparently, the pressure is simply too great. The hero in the Bible epic we're looking at shows us that it can be done. He faced the pressure of success as a young man. This success was to bring him unwanted attention. Let me refresh your memory of the next episode in Joseph's life, as we find it in the book of Genesis, chapter 39. Look out for something that gets repeated a total of four times.

"Now Joseph had been taken down to Egypt; and Potiphar, an Egyptian officer of Pharaoh, the captain of the body-guard, bought him from the Ishmaelites, who had taken him down there. And the LORD was with Joseph, so he

became a successful man. And he was in the house of his master, the Egyptian. Now his master saw that the LORD was with him and how the LORD caused all that he did to prosper in his hand. So Joseph found favour in his sight, and became his personal servant; and he made him overseer over his house, and all that he owned he put in his charge. And it came about that from the time he made him overseer in his house, and over all that he owned, the LORD blessed the Egyptian's house on account of Joseph; thus the LORD'S blessing was upon all that he owned, in the house and in the field. So he left everything he owned in Joseph's charge; he did not concern himself with anything except the food which he ate.

Now Joseph was handsome in form and appearance. And it came about after these events that his master's wife looked with desire at Joseph, and she said, "Lie with me." But he refused and said to his master's wife, "... my master does not concern himself with anything in the house, and he has put all that he owns in my charge. There is no one greater in this house than I, and he has withheld nothing from me except you, because you are his wife. How then could I do this great evil, and sin against God?" And it came about as she spoke to Joseph day after day, that he did not listen to her to lie beside her, or be with her. Now it happened one day that he went into the house to do his work, and none of the men of the household was there inside. And she caught him by his garment, saying, "Lie with me!" And he left his garment in her hand and fled, and went outside. When she saw that he had left his garment in her hand, and had fled outside, she called to the men of her household, and said to them, "See, he has brought in a Hebrew to us to make sport of us; he came in to me to lie with me, and I screamed. And it came about when he heard that I raised my voice and screamed, that he left his garment beside me and fled, and went outside."

So she left his garment beside her until his master came home. Then she spoke to him with these words, "The Hebrew slave, whom you brought to us, came in to me to make sport of me; and it happened as I raised my voice and screamed, that he left his garment beside me and fled outside." Now it came about when his master heard the words of his wife, which she spoke to him, saying, "This is what your slave did to me," that his anger burned. So Joseph's master took him and put him into the jail, the place where the king's prisoners were confined; and he was there in the jail. But the LORD was with Joseph and extended kindness to him, and gave him favour in the sight of the chief jailer. And the chief jailer committed to Joseph's charge all the prisoners who were in the jail; so that whatever was done there, he was responsible for it. The chief jailer did not supervise anything under Joseph's charge because the LORD was with him; and whatever he did, the LORD made to prosper" (Genesis 39:1-23).

It's probably true that how we handle success says as much, if not more, about us than how we handle failure. In order to become equipped to handle even greater responsibility later in life, Joseph was at this stage being challenged with the temptation success can bring. It came about when he was added to Potiphar's collection of servants. Joseph's competence soon caught his master's eye. The Bible record doesn't credit Joseph with this. It tells us the real secret of his competence and success: it lay in the fact that the Lord was with him. I'm sure you picked up on that as the point that was repeated in the Bible story line. It's repeated because this is the big lesson we're meant to learn from Joseph. It's about what God can achieve through us even if we're the most unlikely candidate for success. God's presence in Joseph's life was the difference. Although he'd been torn away from home by family treachery, God was very real to this young man.

It was such an outstanding feature of Joseph's life that it was recognized for what it was by his pagan master. He could see everything that this young man was involved in was blessed as a direct result of his involvement. But promotion for Joseph left him vulnerable to temptation in new ways. Potiphar's wife began to cast longing eyes on this well-built, good-looking young man. Joseph might have been all those things, but he was also a man of powerful convictions. His response is an all-time classic example in overcoming temptation.

Self-gratification comes with a hefty price tag. Joseph saw that. He saw it was wrong ethically and spiritually: for it would hurt others and was against God and all he stood for. Joseph's behaviour also demonstrates a very practical point. Not only did he turn a deaf ear to the woman's advances, he made a special point of avoiding her company so that he'd be less exposed to temptation. A simple story illustrates how the avoidance of danger is the best policy. A Swiss lady once advertised for a chauffeur and received three job applications. She interviewed them individually, each time asking the same question: "How close to a precipice could you drive and still be safe?" The first assured her that he could come within 15 centimetres in complete safety. The second applicant boasted that he could let his outer wheel run on the edge and still have nothing to worry about. The third and last candidate admitted that he didn't know, but that he'd simply prefer to keep as far away as possible. Needless to say, he got the job!

When Potiphar's wife finally got Joseph alone, and he saw what was coming, he simply made a dash to get right out of there. The time for a reasoned defence was over. This was the time to run and it's usually the best defence. Paul told Timothy to 'flee ... youthful lusts'(2 Timothy 2:22). If we allow ourselves to watch every piece of garbage on TV, for example, we shouldn't be surprised to find our resistance to temptation becoming weaker and weaker through exposure to unedifying material.

So how did Joseph clear the hurdle of temptation? By recognizing first and foremost that he belonged to God, that God was with him and by remembering that God had a plan for his life. He also realized the hurt that would be done to others and, especially, that sin is essentially an expression of defiance against God. But Joseph ended up in jail for doing the right thing! Often life isn't fair, but that's no excuse for doing anything other than the right thing. At the end of this incident Joseph again finds comfort in the presence of God. Punished on earth, honoured in heaven; but the divine work in progress in shaping Joseph's character has just taken a major step forward!

9

OVERCOMING DISAPPOINTMENT

We are now at the point where, for no crime other than honouring his master and preserving his sexual purity, Joseph has ended up in prison. I'm reminded of the words the apostle Peter wrote so much later in the Bible - to Christians who were suffering at the hands of the Roman Empire: "It is better, if God should will it so, that you suffer for doing what is right rather than for doing what is wrong" (1 Peter 3:17). Who could have blamed Joseph for wallowing in self-pity at this seemingly cruel turn of events? One thing outstandingly characterizes the life of Joseph as the Bible records it: "the Lord was with him." If other people should turn against him or simply forget him (and we'll see again that they did) Joseph knew that the God who was with him had not forgotten him. Hurt inflicted by others, and the unfairness of life, didn't make him bitter against God, but drew him even closer to the reality of God in his life.

Of course there must have been times when Joseph struggled with the whole thing. We remember that the Bible explains elsewhere that the word of God was testing Joseph. Because of his closeness to God there's every reason to believe that Joseph accepted his circumstances, even to the point of believing his time in prison was by divine appointment. That's the overall perspective we're given. As the next episode now unfolds, we'll be able to glimpse what that divine appointment in the prison was all about:

"Then it came about after these things the cupbearer and the baker for the king of Egypt offended their lord, the king of Egypt. And Pharaoh was furious with his two officials, the chief cupbearer and the chief baker. So he put them in confinement in the house of the captain of the bodyguard, in the jail, the same place where Joseph was imprisoned. And the captain of the bodyguard put Joseph in charge of them, and he took care of them; and they were in confinement for some time. Then the cupbearer and the baker for the king of Egypt, who were confined in jail, both had a dream the same night, each man with his own dream and each dream with its own interpretation. When Joseph came to them in the morning and observed them, behold, they were dejected. And he asked Pharaoh's officials who were with him in confinement in his master's house, "Why are your faces so sad today?" Then they said to him, "We have had a dream and there is no one to interpret it." Then Joseph said to them, "Do not interpretations belong to God? Tell it to me, please. "So the chief cupbearer told his dream to Joseph, and said to him, "In my dream, behold, there was a vine in front of me; and on the vine were three branches. And as it was budding, its blossoms came out, and its clusters produced ripe grapes. "Now Pharaoh s

cup was in my hand; so I took the grapes and squeezed them into Pharaoh s cup, and I put the cup into Pharaoh s hand."

Then Joseph said to him, "This is the interpretation of it: the three branches are three days; within three more days Pharaoh will lift up your head and restore you to your office; and you will put Pharaoh s cup into his hand according to your former custom when you were his cupbearer. Only keep me in mind when it goes well with you, and please do me a kindness by mentioning me to Pharaoh, and get me out of this house. For I was in fact kidnapped from the land of the Hebrews, and even here I have done nothing that they should have put me into the dungeon." When the chief baker saw that he had interpreted favourably, he said to Joseph, "I also saw in my dream, and behold, there were three baskets of white bread on my head; and in the top basket there were some of all sorts of baked food for Pharaoh, and the birds were eating them out of the basket on my head." Then Joseph answered and said, "This is its interpretation: the three baskets are three days; within three more days Pharaoh will lift up your head from you and will hang you on a tree; and the birds will eat your flesh off you."

Thus it came about on the third day, which was Pharaoh's birthday, that he made a feast for all his servants; and he lifted up the head of the chief cupbearer and the head of the chief baker among his servants. And he restored the chief cupbearer to his office, and he put the cup into Pharaoh's hand; but he hanged the chief baker, just as

Joseph had interpreted to them. Yet the chief cupbearer did not remember Joseph, but forgot him" (Genesis 40:1-23).

This encounter with the cupbearer and the baker was the significant thing that happened when Joseph was in the Egyptian prison. It would soon change the course of his life and be instrumental in bringing about a dramatic change in his circumstances. With hindsight Joseph would learn that his meeting in the prison with these two disgraced officials truly was a divine appointment. His encounter with these men was no mere coincidence: it was in the overruling of God. Joseph seemed to be aware of God's control of his life, and that nothing happens purely by chance. The apostle Paul was also someone who had to endure periods of imprisonment. During one of those times, he wrote to Christian friends at a place called Philippi, saying: *"I want you to know ... that the things which happened to me have actually turned out for the furtherance of the gospel, so that it has become evident to the whole palace guard, and to all the rest, that my chains are in Christ"* (Philippians 1:12-13 NKJV).

Accident? No. Divine appointment? Certainly! Was it just that Paul had come to terms with the wrong done to him? No, he actually perceived it had all happened as part of God's plan to get the Christian message to the elite soldiers of the palace guard; people who needed the gospel and with whom he'd never normally have been in contact. Paul speaks about his 'circumstances' or 'the things which happened' to him, but he knew full well that these were not just things which had happened all by themselves. It's a lesson to us that we should look for the hand of God especially in life's unexpected circumstances. We've seen that Joseph and these two disgraced officials had met up in prison right on schedule for the perfect plan of God, even although they wouldn't have chosen those circumstances for themselves. But if God allows difficulties to come into our lives, it's for some positive purpose in the bigger scheme of things.

What can we say about any change we might be able to detect in Joseph while he's still in the prison? One thing that lies on the surface is that Joseph had become sensitive to others. He'd troubled himself to enquire as to the reason why these men were sad. Doesn't this contrast with the insensitivity he'd demonstrated back home when he'd flaunted his dreams - and even his father had been moved to rebuke him? Joseph had enough troubles of his own now; he could have easily ignored the troubles of others. But no, God is changing him on the inside, still at work equipping him for an important work later in life.

However, Joseph's not through with disappointments. Three days later, both dreams came true - events fulfilled them exactly as Joseph had predicted. Great, now surely the butler would repay this kindness by putting in a good word for Joseph with the king! But "the chief butler did not remember Joseph, but forgot him." It's James in his Bible letter who tells us that "the testing of our faith produces endurance" (James 1:3). Patient endurance is to be the first or major result, and that in its outworking can lead to a character that's 'lacking in nothing' (v.4). It's as if James is telling us that the indispensable character quality of patient trust in God can really only be fully learned through trials and difficulties - and that's why God in his often inscrutable wisdom allows these things into our lives. Joseph had overcome treachery, and overcome temptation and now he was overcoming disappointment and in the process he was learning endurance. Overcoming life's disappointments was developing in him a real sense of patient trust in God.

10

OVERCOMING SUCCESS

A man called J. Oswald Sanders once wrote 'not every man can carry a full cup. Sudden elevation frequently leads to pride and a fall. The most exacting test of all is to survive prosperity.' In this latest episode from the life of Joseph we're going to find Joseph facing this most exacting of all tests. We're also going to see that God's patient investment in the life of Joseph was going to pay dividends. Well, we left Joseph in prison - it was where the butler had left him, since for two whole years he'd clean forgotten to pass on Joseph's special plea to Pharaoh. Let's pick up the thread of the story line again:

> *"Now it happened at the end of two full years that Pharaoh had a dream, and behold, he was standing by the Nile. And lo, from the Nile there came up seven cows, sleek and fat; and they grazed in the marsh grass. Then behold, seven other cows came up after them from the Nile, ugly and gaunt, and they stood by the other cows on the bank of the Nile. And the ugly and gaunt cows ate up the seven sleek and fat cows. Then Pharaoh awoke. And he fell*

asleep and dreamed a second time; and behold, seven ears of grain came up on a single stalk, plump and good. Then behold, seven ears, thin and scorched by the east wind, sprouted up after them. And the thin ears swallowed up the seven plump and full ears. Then Pharaoh awoke, and behold, it was a dream. Now it came about in the morning that his spirit was troubled, so he sent and called for all the magicians of Egypt, and all its wise men. And Pharaoh told them his dreams, but there was no one who could interpret them to Pharaoh.

Then the chief cupbearer spoke to Pharaoh, saying, "I would make mention today of my own offenses. Pharaoh was furious with his servants, and he put me in confinement in the house of the captain of the bodyguard, both me and the chief baker. And we had a dream on the same night, he and I; each of us dreamed according to the interpretation of his own dream. Now a Hebrew youth was with us there, a servant of the captain of the bodyguard, and we related them to him, and he interpreted our dreams for us. To each one he interpreted according to his own dream. And it came about that just as he interpreted for us, so it happened; he restored me in my office, but he hanged him."

Then Pharaoh sent and called for Joseph, and they hurriedly brought him out of the dungeon; and when he had shaved himself and changed his clothes, he came to Pharaoh. After Pharaoh had recalled his dreams, Joseph said to Pharaoh, "Pharaoh's dreams are one and the same; God has told to Pharaoh what He is about to do.

The seven good cows are seven years; and the seven good ears are seven years; the dreams are one and the same. And the seven lean and ugly cows that came up after them are seven years, and the seven thin ears scorched by the east wind shall be seven years of famine. It is as I have spoken to Pharaoh: God has shown to Pharaoh what He is about to do. Behold, seven years of great abundance are coming in all the land of Egypt; and after them seven years of famine will come, and all the abundance will be forgotten in the land of Egypt; and the famine will ravage the land.

So the abundance will be unknown in the land because of that subsequent famine; for it will be very severe. Now as for the repeating of the dream to Pharaoh twice, it means that the matter is determined by God, and God will quickly bring it about. And now let Pharaoh look for a man discerning and wise, and set him over the land of Egypt ... Then let them gather all the food of these good years that are coming, and store up the grain for food in the cities under Pharaoh's authority, and let them guard it. And let the food become as a reserve for the land for the seven years of famine which will occur in the land of Egypt, so that the land may not perish during the famine."

Now the proposal seemed good to Pharaoh and to all his servants. Then Pharaoh said to his servants, "Can we find a man like this, in whom is a divine spirit?" So Pharaoh said to Joseph, "Since God has informed you of all this, there is no one so discerning and wise as you are. You shall be over my house, and according to your command all my people shall do homage; only in the throne I will be greater than you." This is what happened, and when the seven years of plenty which had been in the land of Egypt came to an end, and the seven years of famine began to come, just as Joseph had said, then there was famine in all the lands; but in all the land of Egypt there was bread...And the people of all the earth came to Egypt to buy grain from Joseph, because the famine was severe in all the earth" (Genesis 41:1-57).

I've read that Gladstone once said: 'A great statesman is a man who knows the direction God is going for the next 50 years!' Wow, that certainly would be a great statesman! But Joseph through Pharaoh's dream was able to discern by God's help the direction things were headed in over the next fourteen years. By the time Joseph stood before Pharaoh, he'd learned through experiencing treachery, temptation and disappointment - learned through coping with mistreatment, slavery and imprisonment - that God remains in control. He'll do what he promises to do, because ultimately he's in charge. Out of his own steep learning curve, Joseph now invites Pharaoh to acknowledge God's purposes and plan accordingly. Because if God said hard times were going to come to the land of Egypt and beyond, then come they would. To plan ahead would require the Egyptians to be economical during the good years.

This is now the third pair of dreams Joseph has been confronted with. Even when Pharaoh began to ask for Joseph's help, Joseph humbly and properly acknowledged God - he said: "It is not in me; God will give Pharaoh an answer of peace" (Genesis 41:16). 'An answer of peace'- I like that wording. In everything Joseph had been through personally, it seems he'd known at first hand God's answer of peace. If we're facing difficulties right now, we can know the same. Is this not what the Word of God says?

> *"Do not be anxious about anything, but in everything, by prayer and petition, with thanksgiving, present your requests to God. And the peace of God, which transcends all understanding, will guard your hearts and your minds in Christ Jesus"* *(Philippians 4:6–7 NIV).*

When we bring our anxiety to God and present our request to the sovereign Lord of our lives, his first answer to us is peace: the peace of God guarding our hearts in the midst of the storm we're going through. This is the peace that Joseph experienced: the peace to be found in recognizing God's control over the entirety of our life with all its mixed bag of failures and successes. Let's learn together from the way Joseph acknowledges God's sovereignty in personal and international matters. Later on in the story we'll find Joseph expressing very clearly that what had happened to him - beginning with the treachery of his brothers - had all been overruled in God's good purpose to preserve his family through the time of the great famine - and not just his immediate family of course, but the entire nation that would arise from them. How amazing is the detailed care God takes in providing for his people! Finally, didn't Pharaoh hit the nail on the head when he announced that what fitted Joseph most for his new responsibilities was the fact that he was "a man in whom is the Spirit of God" (v.38 NKJV)? Through personal saving faith in Jesus Christ, we too have the Spirit of God residing in our hearts. May he deeply impress on us these wonderful character-building lessons which we can learn from the story of Joseph!

11

OVERCOMING BITTERNESS

Much has happened since Joseph rose to power. The predicted seven years of plenty have come and gone, with Joseph's plan to store up the surplus working out perfectly. It's probably not going too far to imagine Joseph as the second most powerful man in the world at this point in history, as during the following seven years of famine, the surrounding nations came to Egypt - to him - to buy food - including the brothers who had years earlier sold Joseph into slavery. This was a great test of character for Joseph. He recognized them, but they could never have recognized their despised brother in the now grand figure before whom everyone bowed in the land of Egypt.

Safe in his anonymity, Joseph questioned his brothers and discovered that his father and younger brother were still alive. Perhaps he could sense his brothers had changed, but he made sure anyway by putting them to the test. He gave them no alternative but to bring his younger brother Benjamin with them on their second visit. When Benjamin came with them on that second visit, Joseph prepared a banquet for them all. Previously,

Joseph's older brothers had violently resented the favouritism that had been shown to Joseph, so now to test their reaction Joseph appeared to show favouritism to Benjamin by giving him five times as much food as any of the others received. So far so good, the older brothers remained protective of Benjamin. Now Joseph took the test a stage further:

"He commanded his house steward, saying, "Fill the men's sacks with food, as much as they can carry, and put each man's money in the mouth of his sack." And put my cup, the silver cup, in the mouth of the sack of the youngest, and his money for the grain. "And he did as Joseph had told him. As soon as it was light, the men were sent away, they with their donkeys. They had just gone out of the city, and were not far off, when Joseph said to his house steward, "Up, follow the men; and when you overtake them, say to them, 'Why have you repaid evil for good? 'Is not this the one from which my lord drinks, and which he indeed uses for divination? You have done wrong in doing this.'"

So he overtook them and spoke these words to them. And they said to him, "Why does my lord speak such words as these? Far be it from your servants to do such a thing... "With whomever of your servants it is found, let him die, and we also will be my lord's slaves." So he said, "Now let it also be according to your words; he with whom it is found shall be my slave, and the rest of you shall be innocent." Then they hurried, each man lowered his sack to the ground, and each man opened his sack. And he searched, beginning with the oldest and ending with the youngest, and the cup was found in Benjamin s sack. Then they tore their clothes, and when each man loaded his donkey, they returned to the city.

When Judah and his brothers came to Joseph s house, he was still there, and they fell to the ground before him ... Judah said, "What can we say to my lord? What can we speak? And how can we justify ourselves? God has found out the iniquity of your servants; behold, we are my lord's slaves, both we and the one in whose possession the cup has been found." But he said, "Far be it from me to do this. The man in whose possession the cup has been found, he shall be my slave; but as for you, go up in peace to your father." Then Judah approached him, and said, "Oh my lord, may your servant please speak a word in my lord's ears, and do not be angry with your servant; for you are equal to Pharaoh ... our father said, 'Go back, buy us a little food.' But we said, 'We cannot go down. If our youngest brother is with us, then we will go down; for we cannot see the man's face unless our youngest brother is with us.

'And your servant my father said to us, 'You know that my wife bore me two sons; and the one went out from me, and I said, "Surely he is torn in pieces, "and I have not seen him since. And if you take this one also from me, and harm befalls him, you will bring my gray hair down to Sheol in sorrow.' Now, therefore, when I come to your servant my father, and the lad is not with us, since his life is bound up in the lad's life, it will come about when he sees that the lad is not with us that he will die ... For your

servant became surety for the lad to my father, saying, If I do not bring him back to you, then let me bear the blame before my father forever.' Now, therefore, please let your servant remain instead of the lad a slave to my lord, and let the lad go up with his brothers. For how shall I go up to my father if the lad is not with me, lest I see the evil that would overtake my father?" (Genesis 44:1-34).

At this point Joseph was fully convinced his brothers really had changed. He'd appeared to put Benjamin in harm's way in order to test them. They could have either chosen to protect him, or to abandon him just as they had earlier abandoned Joseph. I suppose we could say that Joseph had forced them to revisit the scene of their crime - at least he'd confronted them with the same circumstances. Did they feel a sense of deja vu, I wonder? Would they make the same mistake twice? Would they abandon Benjamin to his fate and return home without him? Well, we've seen that they'd obviously learned their lesson. What's more in the process they confessed their guilt for what they'd done to Joseph. So the same God who'd been developing Joseph's character had clearly also been at work in their lives and consciences.

We've already recalled in this series that Abraham Lincoln, the sixteenth president of the United States, said that it's not so much adversity that's a test of man's character as what he does when he's in a position of power. This was Joseph's great test. As the second most powerful man in the world he could have taken merciless revenge on his brothers. But the extent to which Joseph had overcome any bitterness he might have felt is seen in what actually happened next:

"Then Joseph could not control himself before all those who stood by him, and he cried, "Have everyone go out from me." So there was no man with him when Joseph made himself known to his brothers. And he wept so loudly that the Egyptians heard it and the household of Pharaoh heard of it. Then Joseph said to his brothers, "lam Joseph! Is my father still alive?" But his brothers could not answer him, for they were dismayed at his presence. Then Joseph said to his brothers, "Please come closer to me." And they came closer.

And he said, "l am your brother Joseph, whom you sold into Egypt. And now do not be grieved or angry with yourselves, because you sold me here; for God sent me before you to preserve life. For the famine has been in the land these two years, and there are still five years in which there will be neither plowing nor harvesting. And God sent me before you to preserve for you a remnant in the earth, and to keep you alive by a great deliverance. Now, therefore, it was not you who sent me here, but God; and He has made me a father to Pharaoh and lord of all his household and ruler over all the land of Egypt. Hurry and go up to my father, and say to him, 'Thus says your son Joseph, "God has made me lord of all Egypt; come down to me, do not delay" (Genesis 45:1-9).

The atmosphere must have been electric as forgiveness resolved the issue of guilt. Someone has said, 'Faith lifted the whole sordid crime out of the pit of misery and self-recrimination and placed it on the mountain peak of divine sovereignty where God's forgiving grace not only heals but wipes away the past and the pain' (Unger in his Bible Commentary). Joseph had overcome potential bitterness. Instead, he demonstrated love like that described in First Corinthians 13, love which 'keeps no record of wrongs.' Above all, Joseph could trace the disguised hand of God through everything that had happened. It was really God who'd sent him into Egypt! Joseph cleared life's hurdles because he believed in a God big enough to work through setbacks for the longer-term good of himself and others.

About the Publisher

Hayes Press (www.hayespress.org) is a registered charity in the United Kingdom, whose primary mission is to disseminate the Word of God, mainly through literature. It is one of the largest distributors of gospel tracts and leaflets in the United Kingdom, with over 100 titles and many thousands dispatched annually. In addition to paperbacks and eBooks, Hayes Press also publishes Plus Eagles' Wings, a fun and educational Bible magazine for children, and Golden Bells, a popular daily Bible reading calendar in wall or desk formats.

If you would like to contact Hayes Press, there are a number of ways you can do so:

By mail:c/o The Barn, Flaxlands, Royal Wootton Bassett, Wiltshire, UK SN4 8DY

By phone: 01793 850598

By eMail: info@hayespress.org

via Facebook: www.facebook.com/hayespress.org

About the Author

Born and educated in Scotland, Brian worked as a government scientist until God called him into full-time Christian ministry on behalf of the Churches of God (www.churchesofgod.info). His voice has been heard on Search For Truth radio broadcasts for over 30 years (visit www.searchfortruth.podbean.com) during which time he has been an itinerant Bible teacher throughout the UK. His evangelical and missionary work outside the UK is primarily in Belgium, The Philippines and South East Central Africa. He is married to Rosemary, with a son and daughter.

You can connect with me on:

🔗 https://www.amazon.com/stores/Brian-Johnston/author/B00NPJFXZU

Also by Brian Johnston

Brian has written over 100 books as part of the Search for Truth ministry, across a wide-range of topic - such as evangelism, apologetics, Bible book studies, Bible character studies and core teaching.

Once Saved, Always Saved?
The issue of whether a "born-again" Christian can lose their salvation is an absolutely critical one and has been a controversial topic amongst Christians for centuries. Brian provides a number of faith lessons which include insightful illustrations and Biblical references that all Christians can use to reassure themselves that there is no basis in the Bible for the so-called "Falling Away Doctrine". "For by grace are you saved, through faith."

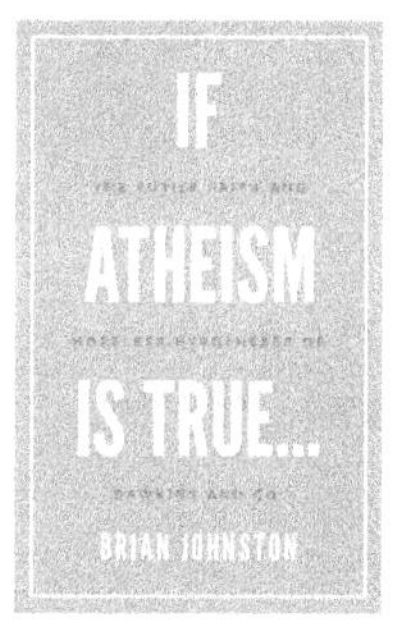

If Atheism Is True...
Written by a former nuclear scientist turned missionary, this book draws together previously published writings on apologetics to produce a concerted offensive against what the apostle Paul would surely describe as the 'indefensible' arguments of the so-called 'New Atheists'.

Finding Christ in the Old Testament

"They said to one another, 'Were our hearts not burning within us when He was speaking to us on the road, while He was explaining the Scriptures to us?'" (*Lk.24:27:32*) Burning hearts! The inevitable result of having the Bible explained so it all begins to make sense and the person and work of Christ, its central character, comes into sharper focus. This book selects and explains 12 Old Testament pictures of Christ.

Knowing God: Reflections on Psalm 23

Psalm 23 is also known as the Shepherd Psalm and it's one of the most-loved passages in the entire Bible. In this book, Bible teacher and radio broadcaster Brian Johnston links in each verse of the Psalm to one of the different names for God that are laid out in the Old Testament - as a great way for us to get to know God better as our PROVIDER, our PEACE, our HEALER, our RIGHTEOUSNESS, as the ONE WHO IS THERE, as the SANCTIFIER, and as SHEPHERD.